Mountains
Surviving on Mt. Everest

by Michael Sandler

Consultant: Daniel H. Franck, Ph.D.

BEARPORT
PUBLISHING COMPANY, INC.

New York, New York

CREDITS
Cover, Lance Trumbull, EverestPeaceProject.org; Title page, Lance Trumbull, EverestPeaceProject.org; 4-5, Ed Webster; 5(R), Lance Trumbull, EverestPeaceProject.org; 6, Steve Stankiewitz; 7, David Beatty/Robert Harding World Imagery/Getty Images; 8, Lance Trumbull, EverestPeaceProject.org; 9, Earth Treks Climbing Centers; 10(L), Gregory G. Dimijian, M.D./Photo Researchers Inc.; 10(R), Aaron Ferster/Photo Researchers, Inc.; 11, Alison Wright/Photo Researchers, Inc.; 12, Lance Trumbull, EverestPeaceProject.org; 13, Paula Bronstein/ Getty Images; 14, AFP/Getty Images; 15, AP Wide World Photos; 16, Lance Trumbull, EverestPeaceProject. org; 17, Lance Trumbull, EverestPeaceProject.org; 18, Ed Webster; 19, Ed Webster; 20, National Geographic/ Getty Images; 21, Ed Webster; 22, Ed Webster; 23, Sevendra Singh/AFP/Getty Images; 24, AP Wide World Photos; 25, Daryl Balfour Gallo Images/Getty Images; 26, Lance Trumbull, EverestPeaceProject.org; 27 AP Wide World Photos.

EDITORIAL DEVELOPMENT by Judy Nayer
DESIGN AND PRODUCTION by Paula Jo Smith

Special thanks for all of their help with this book:
Ed Webster
Lance Trumbull at the EverestPeaceProject.org

Library of Congress Cataloging-in-Publication Data

Sandler, Michael.
  Mountains : surviving on Mt. Everest / by Michael Sandler.
    p. cm.—(X-treme places)
  Includes bibliographical references and index.
  ISBN 1-59716-086-5 (library binding) — ISBN 1-59716-123-3 (pbk.)
1. Sherpa, Temba Tsheri. 2. Mountaineering—Juvenile literature. 3. Wilderness survival—Juvenile literature.
I. Title. II. Series.

 GV200.5.S26 2006
 796.52'2—dc22

                    2005005541

For more information, write to Bearport Publishing Company, Inc., 101 Fifth Avenue, Suite 6R, New York, New York 10003. Printed in the United States of America.

 2 3 4 5 6 7 8 9 10

Contents

Climbing Mount Everest

The clock showed almost midnight. The temperature was freezing. Icy winds roared by.

A group of people huddled in the darkness on a rocky **ridge**. In moments, they would begin the final stage of a dangerous journey. They were climbing to the top of Mount Everest, the world's highest mountain.

Climbing Mount Everest is extremely dangerous. Since 1921, over 180 people have died trying to reach the top.

Among the climbers was Temba Tsheri (SHER-ee) Sherpa. Just two weeks before, Temba had celebrated his 16th birthday. Now he was trying to survive in one of the world's most extreme places. Making it to the top of Everest was Temba's dream. He would be the youngest person ever to reach the **summit**, which is 29,035 feet (8,850 m) high.

Temba Tsheri Sherpa

What Are Mountains?

Mountains are a type of tall landform. They rise high above the area around them. Mountains are taller than hills. They can rise thousands of feet (kilometers) in the air. They are found all over the world, even beneath the sea.

Mountains of the World

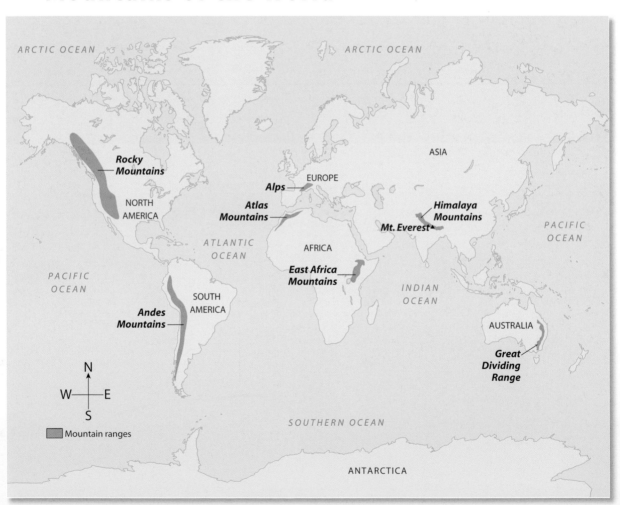

A group of mountains is called a **range**. The biggest mountain range in North America is the Rocky Mountains. The Andes (AN-deez), in South America, is the world's longest mountain range.

Mount Everest, the mountain Temba was climbing, is part of the Himalaya (him-uh-LAY-uh) Mountains. This Asian range is the world's highest. It includes nine of the ten tallest mountains on Earth.

The name "Himalaya" means "home of snow."

Mountains cover one quarter of Earth's land surface.

Mountain Conditions

As Temba approached Everest's summit, survival became harder and harder. Mountain conditions get more extreme the higher a person climbs.

Air contains less and less oxygen as the **altitude** increases. Breathing becomes nearly impossible. Thin air can cause headaches and dizziness at 10,000 feet (3,048 m). Higher up, it can be deadly.

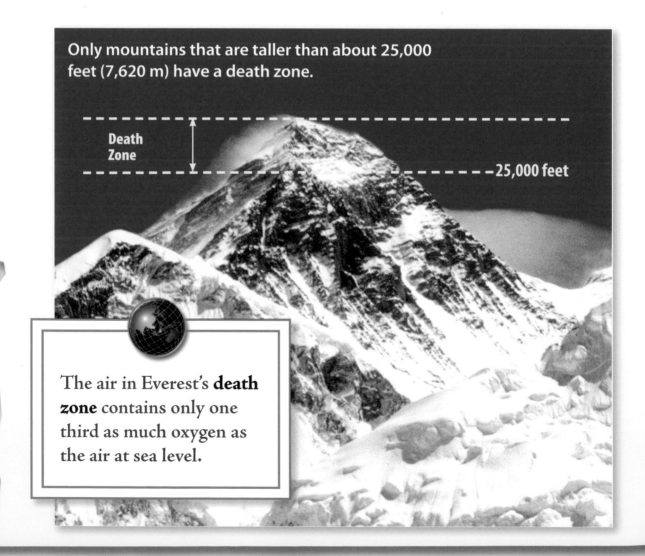

Only mountains that are taller than about 25,000 feet (7,620 m) have a death zone.

Death Zone

25,000 feet

The air in Everest's **death zone** contains only one third as much oxygen as the air at sea level.

The top section of mountains like Everest is called the "death zone." Humans cannot survive here for long. Hurricane-force winds can reach 130 miles per hour (209 kph). Temperatures can **plummet** to -100°F (-73°C) during the night. Blowing snow makes it hard to see. Temba was headed for the death zone.

Death-Zone Survival Equipment

Climbers need a lot of equipment to make the journey up Mount Everest. Here is some of the special gear they need.

Climbing Suit—to protect against extreme cold

Gloves—to keep hands warm and dry

Goggles—to protect eyes from the sun's harmful rays and from reflection off of snow

Oxygen Mask and Tank—for breathing at the highest altitudes

Ice Ax—to help climb slopes and break up ice

Climbing Ropes—to climb up slopes

Trekking Poles—to help a climber stay balanced

Mountain Boots—with spikes that dig into snow and ice

Mountain Wildlife

To survive in the mountains, plants and animals must be **adapted** to the environment. Plants grow close to the ground to keep out of the wind. Small plants grow in the shelter provided by cracks in the rocks.

Mountain cats have large paws and long tails. These features help them keep their balance on **steep**, rocky slopes.

Lichens can grow on bare rocks.

A snow leopard

Yaks are huge, woolly, cowlike animals. Their thick, long hair keeps them warm at high altitudes. To get enough water, they eat snow in the winter.

Few living things can survive at the highest altitudes. At the top of Mount Everest, there is just ice, snow, and rock.

Climbing teams on Mount Everest use yaks to carry supplies such as tents, fuel, and food.

Mountain People

People who live in the mountains must also adapt. They grow crops that can survive in the cold. They raise animals that are suited to the mountain climate.

Temba is a Sherpa, a group of people who live mainly in the Himalayan country of Nepal (nuh-PAL). Sherpas have lived in Nepal's mountains for hundreds of years. They are used to cold temperatures and high altitudes.

Sherpa kids in Nepal

Temba learned the basics of mountain climbing and survival growing up in a Sherpa village in Nepal's Dolakha region. He helped animals graze on steep ground. He hiked on rocky mountain trails to get to his village school.

Sherpas walk for many hours to buy food at this market.

Many Sherpas work as guides for visitors who come to climb Mount Everest.

Why Do People Climb Mountains?

People climb mountains for many reasons. Some enjoy the thrill of being high above the clouds. Others like the challenge of testing their skills.

For decades, however, reaching the top of Everest was a test that no climber could pass. The first attempts to climb Everest were made during the 1920s. Again and again, the climbing teams stopped short of their goal. **Avalanches**, storms, sickness, and exhaustion brought them to a halt.

Avalanches cause more deaths on Mount Everest than anything else.

George Mallory, shown here on a mountain in France, made three attempts to climb Everest. He disappeared near the top in 1924.

Then, in 1953, two climbers finally succeeded—Sir Edmund Hillary and Tenzing Norgay. Sir Hillary was from New Zealand. Norgay was a Sherpa from Nepal.

Sir Edmund Hillary (left) and Tenzing Norgay (right) show off their survival equipment in 1953.

Temba's Mistake

Temba had tried to climb Everest before. It ended, however, in failure.

"I didn't have enough training or proper equipment," Temba said. He was almost at the summit when his oxygen supply ran out.

To reach the top of Everest, Temba needed to have the right equipment. Climbers today carry up to 30 pounds (14 kilograms) of equipment.

Without oxygen, Temba couldn't think clearly. He made a terrible mistake. He took off his gloves to tie his boots. His fingers froze. Temba suffered **frostbite** on both hands. He had to turn back just 70 feet (21 m) from his goal.

The next time around, however, Temba was prepared. He had trained hard. He had the right equipment, thanks to his classmates and teachers. They had raised money for his trip.

Temba lost several fingers on each hand to frostbite.

Frostbite can happen when it's so cold that hands, feet, and other parts of the body freeze solid. Frostbite can cause people to lose fingers, toes—even their noses.

Camp-to-Camp

Temba's second try began in April 2001. Mount Everest sits between Nepal and Tibet (ti-BET). There are several different **routes** to the top. Temba would take a route from the north, the Tibetan side.

A Route to the Top

Summit
29,035 feet (8,850 m)

Camp Five
27,200 ft (8,291 m)

Camp Four
25,500 ft (7,772 m)

Camp Three
23,800 ft (7,254 m)

Camp Two
22,500 ft (6,858 m)

Advanced Base
20,000 ft (6,096 m)

Base Camp
17,500 ft (5,334 m)

Climbers move from one camp to the next higher one and then rest for a while. At each camp, their bodies get used to the higher altitudes. Temba spent several weeks moving between camps with his team.

At Camp 3, the team waited for a break in the weather. Winter was over, but there had been a series of severe snowstorms. Getting caught in a snowstorm farther up the mountain would be deadly.

Tents at base camp

The climb up Everest officially begins at base camp. Climbers stay in tents there so their bodies get used to the lower levels of oxygen.

The Climb Along the Ridge

On May 20, Temba's team reached Camp 4. Then the climbers headed out on the great ridge leading to the summit. Temba plunged his ax into ice walls, pulling himself up. He steadied himself against 50-mile-per-hour (80-kph) winds. Yet, he climbed higher and higher.

Climbers use aluminum ladders to cross deep cracks in the ice, called crevasses. The crevasses are constantly opening and closing, so it's very dangerous.

Temba was in the death zone. He had to move fast or die. Darkness stopped him before he got to Camp 5. His team had gone ahead. Luckily, Temba found a tent. He spent the night frightened and alone.

The next day, Temba rejoined his team. They reached Camp 6, one day's climb from their goal.

Climbers have to be very careful. Towers of ice can fall over without warning.

Most of Everest is covered with ice. Climbers use ropes and ladders to make it through ice fields.

Reaching the Top of the World

Just before midnight, Temba began his final climb. A headlamp lit the darkness. An oxygen mask helped Temba to breathe.

It is dangerous for climbers to spend more than ten minutes at the top of Everest. The body needs to get to a lower altitude, where there is more oxygen.

Rescue teams and helicopters can't reach the top of Everest. If people die near the summit, their bodies have to be left there, frozen.

He passed the frozen body of a climber who hadn't made it. Carefully, Temba pressed on. Sometimes he'd stop to rest or to change oxygen bottles.

Just after sunrise, Temba reached Mount Everest's summit. He was higher than anyone else on the planet.

Temba planted two flags. One was for his school. The other was for Nepal. "I felt so happy," he said.

Temba was the youngest person to climb Mount Everest.

Will the Mountains Survive?

Temba survived in the mountains. Now, he wants to make sure the mountains survive. The world's mountains face many different threats.

Trash is one problem. For a while, Everest was called the "world's highest garbage dump." The mountain was littered with tons of trash that climbers left behind—batteries, bottles, and empty oxygen tanks. Many climbers didn't have the time or strength to carry these things back down with them.

Climbers have left garbage on Everest since 1921.
Now, people are trying to clean up the mess.

Global warming is another problem. As Earth gets warmer, mountain **glaciers** are melting. Himalayan lakes are swelling up with water. When they flood, mountain landscapes will be changed forever.

Mount Kilimanjaro, in Africa

In 2005 the snowcap on Tanzania's Mount Kilimanjaro melted for the first time in history.

After the Climb

When Temba came down from Everest, he was thinking about food, not fame. After weeks of camping, he was starving for home cooking.

Temba returned to Kathmandu after climbing Everest.

Kathmandu (kat-man-DOO) lies in a valley between Himalayan mountains. It is the capital and largest city of Nepal. Most **expeditions** to Everest begin at Kathmandu.

Still, when he flew home to Kathmandu, a huge crowd was waiting. Temba couldn't believe it. "I had never seen so many cameras. . . . All of them were pointed at me," he said.

Despite the attention, Temba focused on his schoolwork. He needed a good education to achieve his other dream, starting a school in Dolakha.

Will Temba succeed? Only time will tell. If you've survived on Everest, however, and reached the top, no goal seems too high!

Temba smiled at supporters who greeted him at the Kathmandu airport after he successfully climbed Mt. Everest.

Just the Facts

MORE ABOUT EVEREST AND MOUNTAINS

- Mountains provide freshwater for over half the people in the world. Water falls on mountains as rain or snow. Then it is stored as snow or ice. When the snow and ice melt, they run downhill in rivers. Most of the world's biggest rivers begin in the mountains.

- The British gave Everest its name in 1865. They named the mountain after Sir George Everest, who mapped the area. However, local people had long used other names for the mountain. The people of Nepal call it Sagarmatha, which means "Forehead in the Sky." The people of Tibet call it Chomolungma, which means "Mother Goddess of the World."

Timeline

The timeline shows some important events in the history of Mount Everest.

1921
A team of British climbers, including George Mallory, makes the first attempt to climb Mount Everest.

1850   1875   1900   1925

1852
A team of scientists determines that Everest, then called Peak XV, is the highest mountain in the world.

1924
George Mallory and climbing partner, Andrew Irvine, disappear near the top of the summit.

- In 1999, Babu Chiri Sherpa became the only person in history to spend a night at the top of Mount Everest. He set a record by staying at the summit for 21 hours.

- Marco Siffredi of France snowboarded down Everest from the north side in two and a half hours in 2001.

- In 1998, Jean-Marc Boivin climbed to the summit. Then he jumped off! He used a winglike parachute called a paraglider to fly down 8,000 feet (2,438 m) in 11 minutes.

- Surprisingly, no one had skied down from Everest's peak to base camp until 2000. That year, Davo Karnicar strapped on his skis at the summit. Then he made the world's ultimate 11,000-foot (3,353-m) ski run.

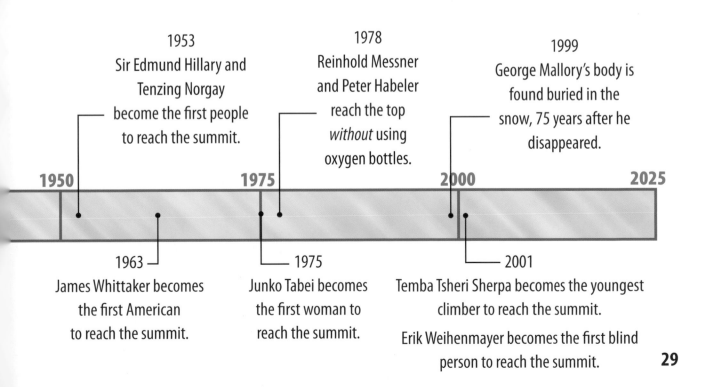

1953 Sir Edmund Hillary and Tenzing Norgay become the first people to reach the summit.

1978 Reinhold Messner and Peter Habeler reach the top *without* using oxygen bottles.

1999 George Mallory's body is found buried in the snow, 75 years after he disappeared.

1950 — **1975** — **2000** — **2025**

1963 — James Whittaker becomes the first American to reach the summit.

1975 — Junko Tabei becomes the first woman to reach the summit.

2001 — Temba Tsheri Sherpa becomes the youngest climber to reach the summit.

Erik Weihenmayer becomes the first blind person to reach the summit.

GLOSSARY

adapted (uh-DAP-tid) changed because of the environment or conditions; changed over time to be fit for the environment

altitude (al-ti-TOOD) the height above sea level

avalanches (AV-uh-lanch-iz) giant amounts of snow or ice that fall down the side of a mountain at great speed and without warning

death zone (DETH ZOHN) the name given to altitudes above 25,000 feet (7,620 m), where humans can live only a short time

expeditions (ek-spuh-DISH-uhnz) long journeys taken for a reason, such as exploring

frostbite (FRAWST-bite) the freezing of skin and flesh due to exposure to extreme cold

glaciers (GLAY-sherz) huge areas of ice and snow found on mountains and near the North and South poles

global warming (GLOHB-uhl WARM-ing) a rise in temperatures around the world

plummet (PLUHM-it) to drop suddenly

range (RAYNJ) a set of mountains that form a group

ridge (RIJ) a long, thin section of a mountain

routes (ROOTS or ROUTS) ways of getting from one place to another

steep (STEEP) sloping up or down very sharply

summit (SUHM-it) the very top of a mountain

BIBLIOGRAPHY

Coburn, Broughton. *Everest: Mountain Without Mercy.* Washington, D.C.: National Geographic (1997).

Price, Martin F. *Mountains.* Stillwater, MN: Voyageur Press (2002).

Rai, Dinesh. "Temba Tsheri: On Top of the World at 16." *Shangri-La In-Flight Magazine* (January 2003).

The Kathmandu Post

The Nepali Times

READ MORE

Chester, Jonathan. *The Young Adventurer's Guide to Everest: From Avalanche to Zopkio.* Berkeley, CA: Tricycle Press (2005).

Jenkins, Steve. *The Top of the World: Climbing Mount Everest.* Boston: Houghton Mifflin (1999).

Levin, Judy. *Life at a High Altitude.* New York: Rosen Central (2003).

Platt, Richard. *Everest: Reaching the World's Highest Peak.* New York: DK Publishing (2000).

Salkeld, Audrey. *Climbing Everest: Tales of Triumph and Tragedy on the World's Highest Mountain.* Washington, D.C.: National Geographic (2003).

Simon, Seymour. *Mountains.* New York: HarperTrophy (1997).

LEARN MORE ONLINE

Visit these Web sites to learn more about Mount Everest:

www.mos.org/Everest/home.htm

www.nationalgeographic.com/everest/

www.pbs.org/wgbh/nova/everest/

INDEX

ABOUT THE AUTHOR

Michael Sandler lives in Brooklyn, New York. He has written many books for children and young adults. A frequent traveler to the world's extreme places, he has visited the Himalayan foothills, though never Mount Everest itself.